There is one person who is the foundation of North Central University. While many persons have invested time and talents in North Central, it is because of one, Jesus, who was born 2,000 years ago that brings us together. It is because of Him that North Central exists in order to prepare people to be dynamic believers wherever God might place them and that they might declare this wondrous story to all who will listen. I trust you will find this book a blessing for your family each Christmas as it celebrates the simplicity and majesty of our Lord Jesus Christ.

Gordon Anderson

THIS BOOK BELONGS TO

_____

_____

DATE

ISBN 1-932458-23-9

Books may be purchased from Bronze Bow Publishing, Inc., 2600 E. 26th Street,
Minneapolis, MN 55406 or call toll free 866-724-8200. You can contact us on
the Internet at www.bronzebowpublishing.com.

All Scripture quotations are taken from the King James Version of the Bible.

This book in its entirety—from literary development to artwork and final design—
is a creation of Koechel Peterson & Associates, Inc., Minneapolis, MN and David
Rose, Editor, CastleRose.

Printed in Mexico

ART: Cover *Holy Night (Adoration of the Shepherds)* by Correggio. © Erich Lessing/Art
Resource • Back cover *The Adoration of the Shepherds* by Adriaen van der Werff. © Arte &
Immagini srl/CORBIS • 2-3 *Madonna and Child with Saint Frances of Rome* by Orazio
Gentileschi. © Arte & Immagini srl/CORBIS • 6-7 *Vanitas with Royal Crown* by Vincent
van der Vinne. • 8-9 *Renaissance Madonna and Child.* © Ali Meyer/CORBIS • 10-11 *Holy
Family* by Raphael. © Scala/Art Resource • *The Holy Family* by Sisto Badalocchio. Wadsworth
Atheneum, Hartford • 14-15 *The Adoration of the Shepherds* by Adriaen van der Werff. ©
Arte & Immagini srl/CORBIS • 16-17 *The Annunciation* by Francesco Albani • 18-19 *The
Immaculate Conception* by Giovanni Battista Tiepolo. © Archivo Iconografico, S.A./CORBIS
• 20-21 *The Communion of the Apostles* by Joos van Ghent. © Alinari Archives/CORBIS
• 22-23 *Hampstead Heath, Branch Hill Pond* by John Constable. © Stapleton Collection/-
CORBIS • 24-25 *Adoration of the Shepherds* by Bartolome Esteban Murillo. © Archivo
Iconografico, S.A./CORBIS • 26-27 *Virgin of the Annunciation* from the *Virgin and Child
with Angels and Saints* Triptych by Fra Angelico. © Alinari Archives/CORBIS • 28-29 *Holy
Family* by Andrea del Sarto. © Araldo de Luca/CORBIS • 30-31 *Mary Magdalen* by Titian.
© Archivo Iconografico, S.A./CORBIS • 32-33 *An Angel* by Guido Reni. © Scala / Art
Resource, NY • 34-35 *Annunciation* by Bartolome Esteban Murillo. © Scala/Art Resource
• 36-37 *Nativity* by Federico Barocci. © Francis G. Mayer/CORBIS • 38-39 *Annunciation
to the Shepherds* by Jacopo Bassano. © Erich Lessing/Art Resource, NY • 40-41 *Adoration
of the Shepherds* by Anton Raphael Mengs. © Scala / Art Resource, NY • 42-43 *Nativity* by
Pedro de Moya. © Archivo Iconografico, S.A./CORBIS • 44-45 *Adoration of the Shepherds*
by Bartolome Esteban Murillo. © Archivo Iconografico, S.A./CORBIS • 46-47 *Virgin and
Child* by Rogier van der Weyden. © Museum of Fine Arts, Houston; the Edith A. and Percy
S. Straus Collection • 48 Leonardo Da Vinci. • 49 *Adoration of the Shepherds* by Michelangelo
Merisi da Caravaggio. © Archivo Iconografico, S.A./CORBIS • 50-51 *Simeon in the Temple*
by Rembrandt van Rijn. © Bildarchiv Preussischer Kulturbesitz/Art Resource • 52-53 *The
Virgin in Prayer* by Sassoferrato. © London/CORBIS • 54-55 *Journey of the Magi* by James
Jacques-Joseph Tissot. © Minneapolis Institute of Arts, The William Dunwoody Fund
• 56-57 *The Magi* by Harry Siddons Mowbray. © Smithsonian American Art Museum,
Washington, DC/Art Resource • 58-59 *Small Cowper Madonna* by Raphael. © Francis G.
Mayer/CORBIS • 60 *The Virgin and Child with Saint Anne and Saint John the Baptist* by
Leonardo da Vinci. © National Gallery Collection; By kind permission of the Trustees of
the National Gallery, London/CORBIS • 61 *The Madonna Litta* by Leonardo da Vinci
© CORBIS • 62-63 *The Flagellation of Christ* by Michelangelo Merisi da Caravaggio.
© Archivo Iconografico, S.A./CORBIS • 64 *The Good Shepherd* by Bartolome Esteban
Murillo. © Archivo Iconografico, S.A./CORBIS

THE
HEART
OF
Christmas

THE COMING *of the* CHRIST CHILD

BRONZE BOW
CASTLEROSE

Heart

Before the Passion of the Christ on Calvary *there was the passion of His birth in Bethlehem.*

A Glorious beginning heralded by angels.

An ignominious end of suffering and betrayal.

All things to the glory of God.

All things for the salvation of man.

A whole story, one that began in the eternal heart of God.

One that ended in the very same place. All in all.

A love story,

THE HEIGHT AND BREATH AND DEPTH OF

JESUS *the Christ Child.*

Jesus the suffering Christ.

THE ONE *and*

ONLY

true Christmas gift.

WHICH ONLY GOD HIMSELF COULD FILL.

Jesus the Christ Child.

Jesus the suffering Christ.

The one and only true Christmas gift.

We have endeavored to honor the great masters of art.

As they sought to honor the only true Master of hearts.

We present the story of Christmas from the words of the Bible—

THE HEART OF CHRISTMAS

Christmas

Most High, glorious God,

ENLIGHTEN THE SHADOWS OF MY HEART,

and grant unto me right faith,

certain hope and perfect charity,

sense and understanding, Lord,

so that I may accomplish

Thy holy and true mandate.

ST. FRANCIS OF ASSISI

AND **God** BECAME MAN...

HIS PASSION BEGINS.

Christmas turns all wise souls from the surface

which is time to the center

which is eternity.

E. MERRILL ROOT

BEHOLD THE
Lamb
OF GOD,

which taketh away

the sin of the world....

the Lamb slain

from the foundation of the world.

JOHN 1:29; REVELATION 13:8

And I will put enmity
between thee and the woman,
and between thy seed
and her seed;
it shall bruise thy head,
and thou shalt bruise his heel.

GENESIS 3:15

The cross *always* stands near the manger.

AMY CARMICHAEL

Hail the heav'nly Prince of Peace! Hail the Sun of Righteousness! Born that man no more may die. Born to raise the sons of earth, Born to give them second birth.

CHARLES WESLEY

For **I** know that my redeemer liveth,

and that he shall stand at the latter day upon the earth:

and though after my skin worms destroy this body,

yet in my flesh shall **I** see God:

Whom **I** shall see for myself,

and mine eyes shall behold, and not another;

though my reins be consumed within me.

JOB 19:25–27

"Glory to the newborn King!"

For unto us a child is born,
unto us a son is given:

and the government shall be upon his shoulder:

and his name shall be called

Wonderful

C O U N

The mighty God

THE
Prince
OF
Peace

The everlasting Father

SELLOR

Of the increase of his government and peace

there shall be no end,

upon the throne of David, and upon his kingdom,

to order it, and to establish it with judgment and with justice

from henceforth even for ever.

The zeal of the Lord of hosts will perform this.

Isaiah 9:6–7

And there shall come forth

a ROD OUT *of the* STEM OF JESSE,

and a BRANCH SHALL GROW OUT *of* HIS ROOTS:

and the SPIRIT *of the* LORD SHALL REST UPON HIM,

the SPIRIT *of* WISDOM *and* UNDERSTANDING,

the SPIRIT *of* COUNSEL *and* MIGHT,

the SPIRIT *of* KNOWLEDGE *and of the* FEAR *of the* LORD;

And in that day

THERE SHALL *be a* ROOT *of* JESSE,

WHICH SHALL STAND *for an* ENSIGN *of the* PEOPLE;

to IT SHALL *the* GENTILES SEEK:

and HIS REST SHALL *be* GLORIOUS.

ISAIAH 11:1-2, 10

But thou,

BETHLEHEM EPHRATAH

though thou be little

among the thousands of Judah,

yet out of thee

shall he come forth unto me

that is to be ruler in Israel;

whose goings forth have been from of old,

from everlasting.

MICAH 5:2

O little town of Bethlehem, how still we see thee lie!

Above thy deep and dreamless sleep the silent stars go by.

Yet in thy dark streets shineth the everlasting Light;

The hopes and fears of all the years are met in thee tonight.

PHILLIP BROOKS

BUT WHEN THE FULNESS
OF THE TIME WAS COME,
GOD SENT FORTH HIS SON,
MADE OF A WOMAN,
MADE UNDER THE LAW,
TO REDEEM THEM
THAT WERE UNDER THE LAW,
THAT WE MIGHT RECEIVE
THE ADOPTION OF SONS.

GALATIANS 4:4–5

And the Word was made flesh,

and dwelt among us,

(and we beheld his glory,

the glory as of the only begotten of the Father,)

full of grace and truth.

JOHN 1:14

AND IN THE SIXTH MONTH

the angel Gabriel was sent from God

unto a city of Galilee, named Nazareth, to a virgin espoused to a man whose name was Joseph, of the house of David; and the virgin's name was Mary. And the angel came in unto her, and said, Hail, thou that art highly favoured, the Lord is with thee: blessed art thou among women.

And when she saw him, she was troubled at his saying, and cast in her mind what manner of salutation this should be. And the angel said unto her, Fear not, Mary: for thou hast found favour with God. **And, behold, thou shalt conceive in thy womb, and bring forth a son, and shalt call his name Jesus.**

He shall be great, and shall be called the Son of the Highest: and the Lord God shall give unto him the throne of his father David: and he shall reign over the house of Jacob for ever; and of his kingdom there shall be no end.

Luke 1:26—33

Then said Mary unto the angel,
How shall this be, seeing I know not a man?

And the angel answered and said unto her, The Holy Ghost shall come upon thee, and the power of the Highest shall overshadow thee: therefore also that holy thing which shall be born of thee shall be called the Son of God. And, behold, thy cousin Elisabeth, she hath also conceived a son in her old age: and this is the sixth month with her, who was called barren. For with God nothing shall be impossible.

And Mary said, Behold the handmaid of the Lord; *be it unto me according to thy word.* And the angel departed from her.

LUKE 1:34–38

nd Mary said,

My soul doth magnify the Lord,

and my spirit hath rejoiced in God my Saviour.

For he hath regarded the low estate of his handmaiden:

for, behold, from henceforth all generations shall call me blessed.

For he that is mighty hath done to me great things;

and holy is his name.

Luke 1:46—49

The MAGNI

FICAT

Very flesh, yet Spirit too:
  Uncreated, and yet born;
    God and man in one agreed,
    Very life-in-death indeed.

Fruit of God and Mary's seed;
  At once impassible and torn
By pain and suffering here below;
    Jesus Christ, whom as our Lord we know.

IGNATIUS *of* ANTIOCH

NOW ALL THIS WAS DONE,

that it might be fulfilled which was

spoken of the Lord by the prophet,

saying, Behold a virgin shall be

with child, and shall bring forth

a son, and they shall call his name

Emmanuel, which being interpreted

is, God with us.

MATTHEW 1:22-23

Uncreated

YET BORN

And it came to pass

The hinge of history

is on the door of a

Bethlehem stable.

RALPH W. SOCKMAN

in those days, that there went out a decree from Caesar Augustus that all the world should be taxed. (And this taxing was first made when Cyrenius was governor of Syria.) And all went to be taxed, every one into his own city. AND JOSEPH ALSO WENT UP FROM GALILEE, OUT OF THE CITY OF NAZARETH, INTO JUDAEA, UNTO THE CITY OF DAVID, WHICH IS CALLED BETHLEHEM; (because he was of the house and lineage of David:) to be taxed with Mary his espoused wife, being great with child. And so it was, that, while they were there, the days were accomplished that she should be delivered. And she brought forth her firstborn son, and wrapped him in swaddling clothes, and laid him in a manger; because there was no room for them in the inn.

LUKE 2:1–7

And there were

in the same country

shepherds abiding in the field,

keeping watch over

their flock by night.

LUKE 2:8

Worship Christ, the newborn

Shepherds, in the field abiding,

Watching o'er your flocks by night,

God with us is now residing;

Yonder shines the infant light:

Come and worship, come and worship,

Worship Christ, the newborn King.

JAMES MONTGOMERY

King

AND *Suddenly* THERE WAS

It came upon a midnight clear,
that glorious song of old,
from angels bending near the earth
to touch their harps of gold:
"Peace on the earth, good will to men,
from heaven's all-gracious King!"
The world in solemn stillness lay
to hear the angels sing.

E. H. SEARS

WITH THE ANGEL

a multitude of the heavenly host

praising God, and saying,

Glory to God in the highest,

and on earth peace,

good will toward men.

LUKE 2:13–14

And it came to pass, as the angels were gone away from them into heaven, the shepherds said one to another, Let us now go even unto Bethlehem, and see this thing

THIS IS CHRI

which is come to pass, which the Lord hath made known unto us. And they came with haste, and found Mary, and Joseph, and the babe lying in a manger.   LUKE 2:15–16

Christ the King

ST THE KING

What child is this, who, laid to rest
On Mary's lap, is sleeping?
Whom angels greet with anthems sweet,
While shepherds watch are keeping?

This, this is Christ the King,
Whom shepherds guard and angels sing:
Haste, haste to bring him laud,
The Babe, the Son of Mary!

And when they had seen it,
they made known abroad
the saying which was told them
concerning this child.
And all they that heard it wondered at those things
which were told to them by the shepherds.
But Mary kept all these things,
and pondered them in her heart.

– LUKE 2:17–19

Go, tell it on the mountain

Over the hills and everywhere

Go, tell it on the mountain,

That Jesus Christ is born.

JOHN W. WORK

And, behold, there was
a man in Jerusalem,
whose name was Simeon;
and the same man was just and devout, waiting for the
consolation of Israel: and the Holy Ghost was upon him.
And it was revealed unto him by the Holy Ghost, that he
should not see death, before he had seen the Lord's Christ.
And he came by the Spirit into the temple: and when the
parents brought in the child Jesus, to do for him after the
custom of the law, then took he him up in his arms, and
blessed God, and said, Lord, now lettest thou thy
servant depart in peace,
according to thy word:
For mine eyes have seen thy salvation,
which thou hast prepared
before the face of all people;
a light to lighten the Gentiles,
and the glory of thy people Israel.

LUKE 2:25–32

And Joseph and his mother marvelled at those things which were spoken of him.

And Simeon blessed them, and said unto

Mary his mother, Behold, this child is set

for the fall and rising again of many in Israel;

and for a sign which shall be spoken against;

(yea, a sword shall pierce through thy own

soul also,) that the thoughts of many hearts

may be revealed.   LUKE 2:33–35

Now when Jesus was born

in Bethlehem of Judaea

in the days of Herod the king,

behold, there came

wise men from the

east to Jerusalem,

saying, Where is he that is

born King of the Jews?

for we have seen his star

in the east, and are come

to worship him.

MATTHEW 2:1–2

So bring Him incense, gold, and myrrh,

Come peasant king to own Him,

The King of kings, salvation brings,

Let loving hearts enthrone Him.

God loved the world

For God so loved the world,

that he gave his only begotten Son,

that whosoever believeth in him

should not perish,

but have everlasting life.

For God sent not his Son

into the world to condemn the world;

but that the world through him

might be saved.

JOHN 3:16-17

HE GAVE HIS SON
that the world might be saved

BUT WE SEE JESUS,

who was made a little lower

than the angels for the suffering of death,

crowned with glory and honour;

that he by the grace of God

SHOULD TASTE DEATH
FOR *EVERY* MAN. *Hebrews 2:9*

O come, let us worship
and bow down:
let us kneel before
the LORD our maker.
For he is our God;
and we are the people of his pasture,
and the sheep of his hand.

Psalm 95:6-7